6/98

15 95

# BUILDING

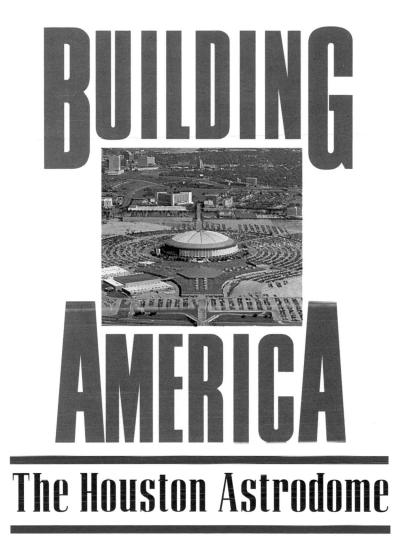

# AMERICA

## The Houston Astrodome

Craig A. Doherty and Katherine M. Doherty

A BLACKBIRCH PRESS BOOK

WOODBRIDGE, CONNECTICUT

**To the memory of our friend, Donna Campbell**

# Special Thanks

*The publisher would like to thank Tara Wenger, reference archivist from the Houston Metropolitan Research Center, Houston Public Library; Jo Gutierrez from the Houston Chronicle Library; Troy Squires from AstroTurf; and Gary Carvey, vice president of engineering, and Lou Callaway from Astrodome USA for their valuable help and cooperation on this project.*

Published by Blackbirch Press, Inc.
260 Amity Road
Woodbridge, CT 06525

© 1997 Blackbirch Press, Inc.
First Edition

Printed in the United States

10 9 8 7 6 5 4 3 2 1

**Editorial Director**: Bruce Glassman
**Senior Editor**: Nicole Bowen
**Associate Editor**: Elizabeth M. Taylor
**Design and Production**: Moore Graphics!

## Photo Credits

Cover and title page: Courtesy of Greater Houston Convention and Visitors Bureau; contents page (from top to bottom): ©Paul S. Howell/Liaison International; Harold Israel/Gulf Photo; AP/Wide World Photos, Inc.; AP/Wide World Photos, Inc.; AP/Wide World Photos, Inc.; page 4: ©Paul S. Howell/Liaison International; pages 6, 22, 32, 34, 35, 37, 40: AP/Wide World Photos, Inc.; page 8: Harold Israel/Gulf Photo; page 10: Collection of the National Baseball Library & Archive, Cooperstown, NY; pages 13, 14, 15 (bottom): ©Houston Chronicle; pages 15 (top), 16, 19, 26, 27, 28, 30, 31: Courtesy Houston Post Collection, Houston Metropolitan Researcher Center, Houston Public Library; page 24: ©Yoichi R. Okamoto/LBJ Library Collection; page 38: Courtesy AstroTurf; page 39: ©Andrew Klapatiuk/Liaison International; page 41: Courtesy of Greater Houston Convention and Visitors Bureau; pages 42–43: ©Bob Thomason/Leo de Wys, Inc.

### Library of Congress Cataloging-in-Publication Data

Doherty, Craig A.
    The Houston Astrodome / by Craig A. Doherty and Katherine M. Doherty.—1st ed.
        p. cm.—(Building America)
    Includes bibliographical references and index.
    Summary: History of the Houston Astrodome, with a focus on its construction and maintenance.
    ISBN 1-56711-113-0 (alk. paper)
    1. Astrodome (Houston, Tex.)—Juvenile literature. [1. Astrodome (Houston, Tex.)
    2. Houston (Tex.)—Buildings, structures, etc.] I. Doherty, Katherine M. II. Title.
    III. Series: Doherty, Craig A.  Building America.
NA6862.U62H685 1997                                                95–25391
725'.827'097641411—dc20                                            CIP
                                                                    AC

# Table of Contents

# Introduction

Just south of the center of Houston—in a spot that used to be part of the flat Texas prairie—lies the Harris County Domed Stadium, better known as the Astrodome. It was the first domed sports stadium and was an engineering marvel when it was built in the 1960s. The story of the Astrodome is also tied to the growth and prosperity of Houston.

Since the discovery of oil in southeast Texas in 1901, Houston has grown to be the fourth-largest city in the United States. It is also the financial, shipping, and manufacturing center of the South. Seven rail lines and nine major highways converge on the city and link up with the 57-mile-long, human-made Houston Ship Channel, which connects Houston with Galveston Bay and the Gulf of Mexico. It is from Houston that NASA (National Aeronautics and Space Administration) tracks and directs the United States' exploration of space.

In the late 1950s, Houston was booming, but a number of people felt that the city was lacking in one respect: It did not have a major league sports franchise. Some of Houston's residents formed a commission and had an $18 million bond passed to provide money for a sports center. (A bond is a device by which government raises money to finance a project and then pays it back with interest.) At about the same time, a group of investors, known as the Houston Sports Association (HSA), set out to bring

**Opposite:**
*The interior of the Astrodome is still impressive 30 years after it first opened.*

*Architect Buckminster Fuller did much to make large dome constructions popular.*

major league baseball to the city. One of the members of the HSA was Judge Roy Hofheinz. Judge Hofheinz brought an interesting perspective to the HSA. He felt that the heat, humidity, and large quantities of rain in Houston during the summer would make it hard to play baseball and attract big crowds.

Judge Hofheinz suggested that the only way baseball would succeed in Houston was if they built a covered stadium and played indoors. No one had ever attempted to build a domed arena of the size Hofheinz envisioned, but he believed that it could be done. Buckminster Fuller, a famous architect and designer of the time, had done a number of experiments with various domed structures and had reportedly told Hofheinz that the size was only limited by the amount of money its builders were willing to spend.

When the Houston Sports Association went to meet with the management and the team owners of baseball's National League in October of 1960, they brought with them a model of the building that Hofheinz envisioned. It is not known how big an impact the domed stadium had on the decision, but the National League granted Houston an expansion-team franchise. The Houston Sports Association now had a team: the Houston Colt .45s—named after the revolver that was carried by many Texans and other westerners during the days of the frontier—but they didn't have a stadium.

It would take several years to build the domed structure, and in the meantime, the Colt .45s needed a place to play. The HSA decided to build a temporary outdoor home for their new ball club. They called it Colt Stadium; it had seating for 32,000 and cost $2 million. Colt Stadium proved Judge Hofheinz's point about needing a dome. The players complained about the humidity and the mosquitoes, while on the muggiest evenings in the summer, the fans stayed home and watched the game on TV from their air-conditioned living rooms.

The financial and engineering obstacles in the way of the domed stadium were many. The bond passed in 1958 was inadequate for covering con-struction expenses, and the way it had been set up made it extremely costly. The members of the HSA lobbied for a new bond issue in Harris County that would refinance the original one and provide enough money to build the Astrodome. There were also legal challenges to the building of a stadium and the granting of the franchise. With backing from the Houston Sports Association, the Harris County commissioners, and the Texas State legislature, the necessary bond issue was passed. The way was clear to build what would be the largest domed structure in the world at the time.

# Building the Dome

 When Judge Hofheinz and the other members of the HSA took the model of their domed stadium to Chicago in 1960, that was all they had. Many people felt that it would be impossible to actually build the Astrodome. In fact, they didn't even get approval from Harris County on the site until August of 1961. The judge, however, believed in the project and called in two Houston architecture firms: Lloyd and Morgan; and Wilson, Morris, Crain, and Anderson. A partner in one of the companies, Ralph A. Anderson, Jr., headed the project and put together a team of designers and engineers that included a physicist, an air-conditioning engineer, an acoustics expert, and designers. They believed that they could come up with a workable design for the stadium the HSA wanted.

# Water, Water Everywhere!

Once the design was completed, the last details for construction could be worked out. For one thing, the ownership of the site had to be finalized. Judge Hofheinz and another member of the HSA, Bob Smith, bought 494 acres from the Hilton Hotel Corporation and combined it with 70 acres that Smith already owned. From this piece of land, 250 acres were to be used for the Astrodome. Hofheinz and Smith paid more than $10,000 an acre and sold the piece for the dome to the county for what they paid for it. Although Smith and Hofheinz made no direct profit on the sale, the HSA was granted a 40-year contract to use and operate the facility. The county also agreed to drain the 70 acres that Smith had owned so that the temporary Colt Stadium could be built.

Water at the site for Colt Stadium was not the only water problem that confronted the builders of the Astrodome. Most of Harris County is less than 50 feet above sea level and is criss-crossed by a number of slow-moving rivers, called bayous. At the official ground-breaking ceremony in January 1962, seven members of the HSA and the county commission fired Colt .45 revolvers into the ground. What they didn't know at the time was that their bullets probably hit water. The construction contract called for the Astrodome's foundation hole to be 26 feet deep and 700 feet in diameter. When that hole was dug, it quickly filled up with water.

Pumping out the foundation hole cost $3,200 a week and held up further construction at the site. The designers solved the problem by devising a permanent drainage system, the cost of which was $288,000. This brought up another issue.

No one knew exactly how much the Astrodome was actually going to cost until all the contractors' bids were in. The low bid came in at $19.44 million, but the county only had $13.4 million left from the $15 million bond issue. In November 1962, the county commissioners approved a $9.6 million supplemental bond, and the voters passed it on December 22, 1962.

*Workers arranged steel reinforcements that formed the base of a 125-foot-high concrete supporting column for the dome's frame.*

## A Sea of Steel

With the money and water problems solved, there was one more detail that needed to be addressed before workers could start erecting the steel to support the roof. In what would eventually be the inside of the dome, 37 towers—varying in height from 185 feet to 202 feet—were constructed to support the

roof temporarily. The towers looked like oil derricks, and some people in Houston thought that the HSA was drilling for oil rather than building a dome! These temporary structures were necessary to support the lamella trusses until they were all in place and connected. Once they were completely interconnected, the lamella trusses would be self-supporting.

With the towers in place, the workers from the American Bridge Division of U.S. Steel began the difficult task of erecting the steel in August 1963. The complexity of the job was due in part to the elaborate design of the lamella trusses and the 642-foot span that the longest truss crossed. Despite the difficulty of the work and the incredibly high heat and humidity, the American Bridge team completed the steel work in only four months.

*Top:*
*Workers began to erect the steel for the walls of the dome during the summer of 1963.*
**Bottom:**
*These support towers were only temporary and were removed once the roof was finished.*

The real test for the roof design came when the temporary towers were taken down. Until they were removed, the ability of the structure to support its 9,000 tons of steel had only been proven in theory by the design engineers. More than 2,890 tons of that steel were in the roof's frame. As the workers started to lower the jacks on the first tower, the roof began to bend out of shape. Everything came to an emergency stop.

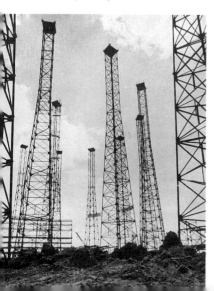

The engineers now had to scramble back to their drawing boards and devise a better way to transfer the weight of the roof from the towers to the tension ring and the supporting frame. After studying the problem, they came up with a series of temporary cross supports. They also decided that all 37 towers would be removed gradually

but at the same time. Once the temporary supports were in place, workers were stationed atop every tower. From there, they simultaneously lowered the jacks one sixteenth of an inch.

Engineers inside and outside the dome watched closely for any further problems. When none developed, they became hopeful and lowered the jacks even further—one sixteenth of an inch at a time. When they finished, the roof was standing free above the towers. By the end of 1963, the steel skeleton was completed, and the task of closing in the dome and finishing the interior could begin.

*Once the outer framework was finished, construction on the interior could begin.*

## Inside and Out

The fact that the stadium was to have a roof created unique opportunities and problems for the designers. The need to escape the heat and humidity of Houston in the summer was the main reason for adding the dome. To make it comfortable inside, however, required a huge air-conditioning system. It was so humid inside that the first time the air-conditioning was turned on, it actually rained indoors!

The total enclosed area of the dome is 405,000 square feet; the heating-and-air-conditioning system cost $4.5 million. This system has a capacity of 6,600 tons and can circulate 2.5 million cubic feet of fresh air per minute. It had to be divided up with separate controls for the upper and lower parts of the stadium. Without the separate controls, the temperature difference between the upper and lower levels might have varied by as much as 50 degrees.

At the time that the dome was built, fans were allowed to smoke cigarettes while watching an event. To prevent the playing field from being hidden in a cloud of smoke, the designers included a sophisticated filtering system for the air inside the dome. It included electrostatic precipitators   devices that gave an electrical charge to the solid smoke particles, causing them to stick to metal plates. After that, the air passed through filters that were so large it took the equivalent of three railroad boxcars of charcoal to fill them. At the time, they were the largest such filters ever made.

The skylights were designed to allow enough light in so a grass playing field could be installed. Not just any grass, however, would grow under these conditions. Scientists at Texas A & M University did a number of experiments on different types of grasses to see which would grow best inside the dome. After a number of trials, a Bermuda-grass hybrid called Tiffway was determined to be the most likely to survive under the reduced light conditions.

Enough grass was planted at the university's turf farm to sod the entire field, but, before final approval was given, the new baseball team went and worked out on it. The people at Texas A & M wanted to see if Tiffway would hold up to the abuses of spiked shoes and game-type situations. The grass passed all the tests and was laid down as soon as the air-conditioning system was turned on. (The scientists who had worked to select the grass felt that the extreme humidity inside the dome before the air-conditioning system was turned on would have killed the turf.)

Now that they had settled on a playing surface, the designers and the construction crews could work on finishing the interior. In outdoor stadiums, the seating materials must be able to withstand all types of weather: sun, heat, rain, cold, wind, and—in much of the United States—snow. The Astrodome designers, however, did not have to worry about weather, so they chose padded and upholstered, theater-type seats. These seats were also brightly colored to give the inside of the dome a more festive feeling. Covering them required more than 45,000 square yards of fabric—a strip 35 inches wide and 25 *miles* long! For people willing to pay the premium price, the Astrodome was the first stadium ever to include luxury boxes, also called sky boxes.

One of the most interesting features of the Astrodome is the moveable seating that allows the grounds crew to change the stadium from a baseball diamond to a football field. The sections of seats that run along the first and third baselines of the baseball field are on tracks. A ten-horsepower motor is attached to each of the two moving sections, and they swing them from parallel to the baselines to parallel to the sidelines of the football field. This gives the Astrodome room for 54,000 baseball fans and more than 63,000 for football. When additional seats are added in the playing-field area, more than 70,000 people can attend a concert.

With an air-conditioned environment and comfortable seats taken care of, the designers worked on providing for the other needs of the people attending events. They added 49 concession stands—spread throughout the 6 levels of the dome—and 4 full-service restaurants. Among the restaurants is the Astrodome Club, which is a private facility that seats

*Not only were the Astrodome's seats designed to be moveable, they were also brightly colored.*

# The First . . . , the Largest . . .

In true Texas style, the Astrodome has boasted a number of records. Among them:

- It was the first fully air-conditioned, enclosed, domed sports arena.
- It was the first stadium with its own weather station on top.
- It contains the first human-made grass field—AstroTurf.
- It was the first domed structure with a span of more than 400 feet (it's 642 feet).
- It has the longest major league baseball dugouts.
- It has the longest and largest scoreboard—474 feet long and half an acre in size!
- It has the largest capacity ice machine in the United States—it can produce 18 tons of ice a day.

600 people for the use of season-ticket holders. In addition to food services, the designers incorporated more than 150 restrooms in their plans.

Acoustics created another set of design challenges. Critics of the dome forecasted that it would become an echo chamber and deafen the people attending events held inside. Acoustically, the dome's shape was perfect, but these deafening predictions would have come true had the designers not planned for the sound problem.

The ceiling of the dome is almost half skylights, while the other half is lined with a special acoustical coating that absorbs sound. The sound reflection qualities of the skylights were taken into consideration when the designers decided how to arrange them. In addition, the lower third of the dome's walls were covered with sound-proofing wood panels. Possibly the most amazing acoustical aspect of the design is the seating. Each folding seat in the Astrodome has shock absorbers built into it to help muffle the noise created by thousands of screaming fans.

The sound system also had to be designed with care. There are 13 huge speakers that hang from the top of the dome. The speakers are controlled by a computer that times the transmissions of sound to prevent feedback. Although Judge Hofheinz's claim that the Astrodome was going to be the quietest stadium around may have been a bit of an exaggeration, the work of the acoustical experts was ultimately quite successful.

The dome's design required a great deal of planning for the movement of people, both inside and outside. The county worked hard to upgrade the road system that would carry the fans to and from the Astrodome. Today, 12 access roads provide 70 lanes of traffic, and the 25,000-vehicle parking lot can be emptied in 20 minutes. The building itself was designed to easily handle the flow of people. Since the playing field is below ground level, people move to the exits from two directions instead of just down as in aboveground stadiums. After the last out in a baseball game, it takes only nine minutes for the fans to leave the dome.

Once spectators are outside, they head for their cars—or to their helicopters if they happened to have used the dome's heliport. There is even a special railroad siding one mile away in case anyone comes to an event in a private railroad car. The movement of all these people and automobiles is directed from an observation post on the highest point of the dome. From this perch, the traffic coordinator is in constant radio contact with the traffic directors in the parking lot and can send traffic away from any problems that develop.

# Play Ball!

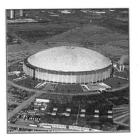

Before the Astrodome opened for the first exhibition game on April 9, 1965, the Colt .45s needed to find a different name. The new president at Colt Industries wanted a share of the profits from the use of his company's name. Rather than cut Colt in on the profits, Judge Hofheinz and the other members of the HSA decided to think of something else to call the team. NASA's Manned Spacecraft Center had opened in Houston in 1961, and that was the inspiration for the new name. The Colt .45s became

*Opposite:*
*This photo from 1965 shows the Astrodome in the year it opened.*

**23**

*U.S. President Lyndon Johnson (left) and Judge Hofheinz (right) watched the opening game on April 9, 1965*

the Houston Astros (*Astros* is short for *astronauts*), and the Harris County Domed Stadium became—unofficially—the Astrodome.

Now that the team had a space-age name for their space-age stadium, they were ready to begin the 1965 baseball season in their new home. President Lyndon B. Johnson, a Texan, was there for the grand opening along with the governor of Texas and the governor of the Mexican state of Tamaulipas.

# SPECTATING IN STYLE

No one considers building a new stadium today without a large number of luxury sky boxes. When the Astrodome was built, the first 54 sky boxes ever put into a stadium were added and paid for by the HSA. The largest was Judge Hofheinz's private apartment. The other 53 boxes were leased out to wealthy businesses and individuals in Houston. The leases ran for five years, and the cost was based on how many seats they had for viewing the events. In 1965, the smaller boxes had 24 seats and cost $15,000 a year, while the 30-seat boxes cost $18,000 a year.

Each box had large adjoining rooms for entertaining. They were decorated in a variety of styles and themes, and each box had a name that fit its decor, such as Las Vegas, New England, Old South, and Egyptian Autumn. All the rooms had closed-circuit TVs for viewing the events, and many of the boxes had stock prices displayed constantly so that those attending the events could keep up with their investments. The boxes also had many other luxury features: Private elevators and special food-and-beverage services were all part of the lease price. When the dome was renovated in 1988 and 1989, an additional 66 new boxes—called Star Columbia Suites—were placed on the club level.

President Johnson watched the game from Judge Hofheinz's private apartment high above right field. There were also many other well-known people in attendance at those first exhibition games.

More than 200,000 fans went through the gates of the Astrodome that weekend. Mickey Mantle of the visiting New York Yankees started off the opening game with a single, which earned him the honor of being the first baseball player to get a hit in the Astrodome. Later in the game, Mantle hit a solo home run, also an Astrodome first. But the Houston Astros won the game 2–1, and everything looked great for the upcoming season.

*The opening of the Astrodome made headlines around the world.*

## Too Much Light

One unforeseen problem began almost immediately upon beginning play in the dome: Seeing high fly balls in the Astrodome outfield was next to impossible on sunny days. The glare from the skylights caused the fielders to lose sight of the ball. An appeal went out to the public for answers on how to solve the problem. One person suggested filling thousands of balloons with helium and releasing them just before the game so that they would block the sun from shining through the skylights. Another person advised that, during day games, they position a blimp so its shadow would fall on the skylights.

Many suggestions were sent in, but the one that seemed the most practical came from greenhouse owners. Greenhouse operators often whitewash the glass in their windows to cut down on the light coming in, and they thought the same could be done for the skylights in the roof of the Astrodome. The problem came to a crisis when on May 23, 1965, the Astros center fielder lost a routine fly ball in the glare and failed to catch it. Three runs were scored, and the Astros lost the game. The next day, workers scrambled over the top of the dome, spraying 700 gallons of an off-white acrylic paint on the skylights. Light transmission was cut in half, and during the next day game, the players reported that the problem had been solved.

*Filled to capacity for a baseball game, the Astrodome can hold 54,000 spectators.*

# AstroTurf

Painting the skylights fixed one problem but caused another: The grass died. For the rest of the 1965 season, the Astros played on dead turf. Before the games, the grounds crew would actually go out and spray the dead grass green! Halfway through the season, the field was pulled up and new turf was laid down. The new turf quickly died and also had to be painted green before the games.

While this was going on, a group of scientists at Chemstrand were hard at work on a solution to the problem. Many chemical companies were trying to create synthetic playing surfaces, but the market was slow in developing. The high price—one to three dollars a square foot—made it hard for organizations to justify the initial cost. The Astrodome had no choice in the matter. When Chemstrand had its artificial turf ready, it was installed in the dome and marketed as AstroTurf.

The Astrodome chalked up another record when the first major league baseball game to be played entirely on artificial turf was held on July 19, 1966. The installation of AstroTurf in the dome—and then in many other stadiums—however, brought up a controversy. Many believe that more player injuries occur on artificial surfaces than on grass. They think that artificial-turf injuries occur because the surface does not give when a player plants his or her foot and makes a sudden change of direction. For this reason, some open-air stadiums that had gone to artificial playing fields have gone back to grass. However, for the 11 domed stadiums that now exist in the United States and Canada, artificial turf is a must.

When the dome's grass died in 1965, workers had to spray it green before each game.

# Up in Lights

The original scoreboard in the Astrodome was so large that it cost more than $2 million. Two companies built the four-story-tall, 474-foot-long, 300-ton machine. It took more than 1,200 miles of wire just to hook up the scoreboard's 50,000 lights!

Before it was replaced in 1988, the scoreboard required a crew of seven technicians to operate the 25-foot-long control panel. They worked in a booth behind home plate so they could watch the game and display appropriate graphics.

Much of the work of animating the scoreboard took place before game time. Designers would create black-and-white cartoons that they felt might work with the sports events. These cartoons would be recorded on film and then, during the game, would be projected on a large screen in the control booth. The screen was composed of a series of switches, which would turn on the corresponding lights on the giant scoreboard when they were hit with light.

During the renovations of 1982, a DiamondVision screen was added to the scoreboard. Then, in 1988, the entire scoreboard was replaced by two giant DiamondVision screens. DiamondVision allows the people in the control panel to transfer video images to the large screens. The video images that are displayed can be from tapes or live from the TV cameras around the dome. Anything that can be recorded on videotape can be displayed on the Diamond-Vision screens. Replays are often shown, and it is not uncommon to see players on the field look up at the screens to see themselves.

*When the Astrodome opened, its scoreboard was the largest and the longest in the world.*

## Hofheinz Takes Over

Although the opening of the dome was a great success from the fans' point of view, there were problems among the people who ran the HSA. The two main partners, Judge Hofheinz and Bob Smith, were no longer getting along. In 1966, Smith gave Hofheinz an ultimatum: sell out or buy out Smith's interests in HSA. Hofheinz had to scramble to come up with the $7 million that Smith demanded for his share, but he was able to buy out his long-time partner and become the principal owner of HSA. It seemed only right that the man who had the original vision to build a domed stadium ended up in almost sole control of it.

*Judge Roy Hofheinz (left) and Bob Smith visit the Astrodome before their business partnership ended in 1966.*

# Astro-Everything

Between 1965 and 1968—the first three years that the Astrodome was in full operation—12 million people passed through its gates. This included 1.5 million who paid one dollar just to walk through when there was no event taking place. The Houston Astros, despite a poor record on the field, had excellent attendance figures, and they were only a small part of the show. Traditionally, the Houston Oilers and the University of Houston football teams also used the dome as their home fields.

## Pitch, Pass, Punch, Polo, and More

Over the years, many forms of sporting events and other entertainment have been held at the Astrodome. In 1967, the dome set the attendance record for an indoor boxing match when Mohammed Ali defeated Ernie Terrell in front of 37,321 fans. The

*Opposite:*
*The Astrodomain complex: In the upper left are Astroworld and Astrobridge.*

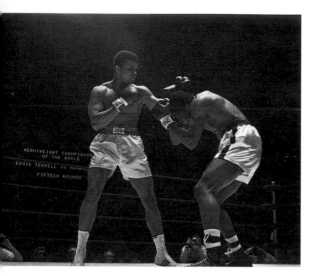

*Mohammed Ali (then called Cassius Clay) won his fight with Ernie Terrell (right) in the Astrodome in February 1967.*

largest crowd ever to watch a regular season college basketball game—52,693 people—saw the University of Houston Cougars defeat the UCLA Bruins on January 20, 1968.

The dome also hosts rodeos, horse shows, soccer games, concerts, and conventions. One of the most important conventions to be hosted by the Astrodome was the 1992 Republican National Convention, which nominated Texan President George Bush to run for re-election. In addition to all this, the dome has seen motorcycle races, auto thrill shows, hockey games, and curling matches.

## Astrodomain, Astrohall, Astrobridge, Astroworld

Judge Hofheinz wanted the Astrodome to be the center of a vast array of activities and amusements. In 1968, a 58-acre amusement park called Astroworld was opened across the highway from the dome. To get to the amusement park, a 532-foot-long bridge—Astrobridge—was built. The bridge includes reflecting pools, antique street lamps, and numerous plantings. The main attraction at Astroworld is Astroneedle, a 340-foot-tall tower. Passengers ride up and down in an elevator that circles the tower twice each way.

From the top of Astroneedle, one can see the entire Astrodomain, which includes the Astrodome, Astrobridge, Astroworld, Astro hotels and motels, and Astrohall/Astroarena complex. The hall/arena is

# THE MAN BEHIND THE DOME

Behind most amazing accomplishments is an amazing person. The man behind the Astrodome was Judge Roy Hofheinz. He was the son of a laundry-truck driver who, through hard work and determination, became wealthy. Hofheinz was born in 1912 and, by the age of 19, was practicing law. At 22, he was elected to the Texas State legislature, and he became a Harris County judge at age 24.

After being a judge, Hofheinz served two terms as Houston's mayor. He was responsible for helping the city modernize. The judge was also Lyndon Johnson's campaign manager when Johnson first ran and was elected to the U.S. Senate. Lyndon Johnson later became president of the United States. When Hofheinz was defeated for his third term as mayor, he chose to end his political career and concentrate on increasing his personal wealth. Prior to joining the group that built the Astrodome, he owned a number of radio and TV stations.

When the Astrodome was built, one of its most interesting features was rarely displayed to the public: the judge's private apartment. It took up almost 17,000 square feet on four different levels and was lavishly decorated with each room done according to a specific theme. One theme that was echoed in the apartment and elsewhere was the judge's ongoing fascination with the circus.

In 1967, when John Ringling North put the Barnum and Bailey's, Ringling Brothers Circus up for sale, the judge agreed to pay $10 million for a 50 percent share of the "Greatest Show on Earth." It seemed appropriate that the man responsible for building one of America's greatest show places, for a time, owned the world's best-known show.

*Judge Hofheinz is shown here in one of the Astrodome's circus rooms.*

the world's largest exhibition and convention center. The hall has 550,000 square feet of floor space; the arena 350,000 square feet. Numerous conventions and exhibits have been held in the $8 million Astrohall/arena since it was first used for the Houston livestock show and rodeo in February 1966.

Judge Hofheinz and his partners made the Astrodome the center of a very successful entertainment and business destination. There is no show or convention too big to fit into the Astrodomain.

# Keeping the Astrodome in Shape

Although the Astrodome was the most advanced stadium in the world when it opened in 1965, it has needed renovating and modernizing twice since then. In 1982, a total of $42 million was spent on improvements that included adding a DiamondVision screen to the scoreboard. Just six years later, in 1988, another $60 million was spent to update many of the features of the dome. Fifteen thousand additional seats were added, in part by tearing out the huge apartment that had originally been built for Judge Hofheinz.

**Opposite:**
*The Astrodome in 1992, at the time the Republican National Convention was held there.*

**37**

During these renovations, the original scoreboard was replaced by two DiamondVision screens. In addition to the two main screens, a number of smaller scoreboards and message boards were installed around the dome.

The most important change for the athletes who play in the dome was the replacement of the original AstroTurf. It had become worn, and advances had been made in the manufacture of artificial grass. In 1988, the AstroTurf in the dome was considered the worst playing surface in the N.F.L. As part of the renovations, a new turf rug for the dome was purchased. In fact, two separate surfaces were created for the dome by AstroTurf Industries, Inc. It was

*The Houston Oilers played football in the Astrodome.*

# THE OTHER DOMES

In 1969, Judge Roy Hofheinz speculated that no other domed stadiums would be built. He felt that increasing costs would make copying the Astrodome economically unfeasible. The judge was partially right because, despite the success of the Astrodome, it was ten years before the next dome was built. He was also right about the cost. The Superdome in New Orleans was the second large domed stadium built and cost nearly $180 million. The Superdome is so big that the entire Astrodome could fit inside it.

Despite the rising cost of building domes, cities around North America continued to do so. Montreal in Quebec, Canada, was next when it built a dome for the 1976 Summer Olympics. Problems with Olympic Stadium's retractable roof, which never worked properly, raised the cost of that stadium to more than $600 million. There are now 11 domed stadiums in North America; the crown jewel of those is Skydome in Toronto in Ontario, Canada.

Skydome cost $583 million to build in 1989, and it has set a new standard for sports and entertainment stadiums. It features a retractable roof, which allows games to be played under the open sky when the weather is nice. If it rains or is too cold or hot outside, the roof can be closed for all the advantages of a domed stadium. The other amazing features of Skydome include a shopping mall, 5 restaurants, and a 350-room hotel. People sitting at a table in the Hard Rock Cafe high above right field can watch a game or concert. The rooms of the hotel also look out over the playing field.

In Pontiac, Michigan, the Silverdome went in a different direction.

The owners built a football stadium that would seat more than 80,000 people and then put a translucent fiberglass dome over it. The only thing holding up the Silverdome's roof is air pressure. Giant fans blow air into the dome so that the air pressure inside is higher than the air pressure outside. This force supports the roof, which is like a huge balloon.

Despite the high cost of building and operating domed stadiums, they have become a symbol of status and economic prosperity for big cities. There are also rewards for these cities. It has been estimated that, despite the fact that the New Orleans Superdome loses approximately $9 million a year, in its first ten years of operation it had a $2.7 billion positive impact on the city's economy. Domes are seen as such important economic stimuli to their communities that the city of St. Petersburg, Florida, built a dome in 1988 even though it had to wait until 1995 before getting a team to play in it. There are still other cities that are talking of building domes, and more are sure to come in the future.

*Toronto Skydome*

decided to have separate football and baseball rugs, which would eliminate the need for a number of the seams that had caused problems in the old surface. Having two turfs would allow the surfaces to be made with the lines as a permanent feature. The new AstroTurf is much better than the original and has more padding underneath to cushion the forces that impact the athletes who play on it.

The renovations, completed in 1989, have made the Astrodome comparable to other more modern stadiums. Increasing the seating, adding more sky boxes, improving the playing surface, and putting in a new scoreboard have greatly improved its usefulness. Along with Astrohall and Astroworld, the Astrodome will continue to be one of America's premier sites for business and entertainment the year round.

*Opposite:
After renovation,
the Astrodome
had one surface
for baseball and
one for football.
Here, the
baseball surface
is in place.*
**Bottom:**
*The impressive
expanse of
Astrodomain can
be seen from high
above Houston.*

*Even today, the Astrodome remains one of the world's greatest feats of engineering.*

# GLOSSARY

**acoustics** The qualities that determine the ability of an area to reflect or absorb sound.

**architect** A person who designs buildings and other structures.

**articulated joint** A joint that can move in more than one direction.

**AstroTurf** The brand name of a carpet made of artificial fibers used to replace grass in sports arenas and other places.

**beam** A long narrow piece of steel used in building a structure.

**bond** A device used by government in which money is raised to finance public projects and then paid back with interest.

**drainage system** A network of underground pipes designed to keep water away from a given site.

**electrostatic precipitator** A pollution control device that is used to remove solid particles from emissions into the atmosphere.

**foundation** The base of a structure that supports the upper portions.

**lacing** The pattern of cross supports in a lamella truss.

**lamella truss** Interconnected series of steel beams that supports the roof of the Astrodome.

**Lucite** The clear acrylic used in the skylights of the Astrodome.

**NASA (National Aeronautics and Space Administration)** The federal agency that is in charge of all U.S. space flights.

**patent** Protection granted to an inventor that allows that person exclusive rights to use or sell his or her invention for a set period of time.

**physicist** A scientist who studies and applies the rules of the physical world.

**scale model** An exact copy of an object that has been reduced in size.

**sky box** Private seating area in front of rooms used to entertain guests during an event.

**skylight** An opening in a roof that is usually covered with glass or transparent plastic.

**sports franchise** Organization that creates and sells teams to companies that then run them.

**tension ring** The 300-ton circle of steel that rests atop the walls of the Astrodome and supports— and holds down—the roof.

**wind tunnel** A mechanical device used to test scale models to see how they will react to strong winds.

# CHRONOLOGY

**1958 February 10**—Commission created to study building a new sports facility.

**July 26**—Voters approve an $18 million bond issue.

**1960** Hofheinz and Smith become involved in the project.

**October 17**—Model of proposed domed stadium shown to National League owners.

**October**—The National League grants the Houston Sports Association a franchise for a major league baseball team.

**1961 January**—A new bond issue is passed to reflect expected higher costs of building a domed stadium.

**May 9**—County selects architectural firms to complete the design work on the dome.

**August 28**—Land deal for the dome's site is finalized.

**September**—New cost estimates indicate more money is needed.

**Contract** between the HSA and the county is signed for the operation and management of the dome.

**1962 January 3**—Ground-breaking ceremony is held at the site.

**June to December**—Excavation company requires additional money to pump out ground water.

**December 22**—Supplemental bond issue passes.

**1963 May**—Work on foundation begins.

**July**—U.S. Steel begins work on skeleton of the dome, and towers to support the roof during construction are moved into place.

**August**—Work begins on actual dome.

**November 1**—Steel work is completed.

**December 2**—Towers are removed.

**1964 March**—Ramps and exterior trim are added; stands are begun.

**August 18**—Stadium is completed except for finishing details.

**October 1**—Colt .45s baseball team changes name to the Astros.

**December 13**—The Harris County Domed Stadium unofficially becomes the Astrodome.

**1965 April 9**—Grand opening of the Astrodome; first indoor baseball game played.

**1982** Renovations done.

**1988–89** Interior renovations; new artificial surfaces for both baseball and football installed.

**1995 April 9**—30th anniversary of the Astrodome.

# FURTHER READING

*There are currently no books in print about the Astrodome suitable for young adult readers. In fact, there are no books in print about the Astrodome for any readers. The following are on related topics for young readers.*

Boring, Mel. *Incredible Constructions and the People Who Built Them.*
　　New York: Walker & Co., 1985
*"Dome."* MS Encarta. CD-ROM, 1994.
Lambert, Mark. *Building Technology.* Chicago: Franklin Watts, 1991
Marsh, Carole. *Texas Timeline*: A *Chronology of Texas History, Mystery, Trivia,*
　　*Love, and More.* Decatur, GA: Gallopade Pub. Group, 1992.
Morgan, Sally and Adrian Morgan. *Structures.* New York:
　　Facts On File, 1993.
Stein, R. Conrad. *Texas.* Chicago: Childrens Press, 1989.

# SOURCE NOTES

Astor, G. "Pop Goes the Ball Game." *Look.* August 8, 1967, v. 31, 52–3.
"Astrodome's Top 10 Moments Uncovered." *Houston Post.* April 8, 1990.
Callaway, Lou. "Astrodome Facts." Astrodome USA.
Cartwright, Gary "Barnum Named Hofheinz." NY *Times Magazine.* July 21, 1968, 10.
Conniff, Richard. "After a While, Nothing Seems Strange in a Stadium with a Lid." *Smithsonian.*
　　January 1988, 114.
"The Dome at 25." *Houston Post.* April 9, 1990.
"Domes Stadium." U.S. *News and World Report.* October 11, 1965, 59:10.
Duffey, Gene. "Old-timers Remember Dome's Good Old Days." *Houston Post.* April 9, 1990.
"Eighth Wonder 25 Today." *Houston Post.* April 9, 1990.
Ellison, David. "Astrodome Turf Scores with Athletes." *Houston Post.* January 14, 1988.
"Farewell to Grass." *Newsweek.* May 11, 1970, v. 75, 73.
Flood, Mary. "Wonder of Wonders Celebrates Its 25th." *Houston Post.* April 8, 1990, A-1.
Frady, Marshall. "Hofheinz and the Astrodome." *Holiday.* May 19, 1969, v. 45, 42–5.
"Greatest Show on Earth." *Time.* November 27, 1967, 90:98.
"Happy Birthday, Old Dome." *Newsweek.* April 15, 1985, v. 105, 11.
"Here Comes the Judge." *Newsweek.* May 27, 1968, 71:74–74A.
Herskowitz, Mickey. "Dome Hits 30." *Houston Post.* April 9, 1995.
———."Hofheinz Dome Home to Go." *Houston Post.* March 15, 1988, A-1.
"Home in the Dome." *Sports Illustrated.* August 16, 1994, 42.
"Houston Gets a New Astrowonder." *Business Week.* June 8, 1968, 88.
Houston, *Texas Astrodome and the Astrodomain.* Houston, TX: Astrodome, USA, 1975.
Jares, J. "Big Screen Is Watching." Sports Illustrated. May 31, 1965, 22:30–1.
McDermott, J. R. "What a Wonder." *Life.* April 23, 1965, 58:76–8.

McCarthy, Paul. "Artificial Turf." *Physician & Sports Medicine*. October 1989, v. 17, n. 10, 158–162.

McLemore, Ivy. "Grand Lady of the Domes Candidly Aware of Her Role in Sports History." *Houston Post*. April 8, 1990.

———."New-look Dome in Store for Astro's Fans This Year." *Houston Post*. April 4, 1988.

———."Old Astrodome Scoreboard to Live on." *Houston Post*. January 10, 1988, C-8.

Maule, T. "Greatest Showman on Earth." *Sports Illustrated*. April 21, 1969, 30:37–8.

Olafson, Steve. "Dome's Birthday Celebration Has It All." *Houston Post*. April 10, 1985, A-1.

"Outdoor Sports with Indoor Comfort." U.S. *News and World Report*. February 22, 1965, 58:16.

Petty, John Ira. "Those Folks who Built the Incredible Dome." *Houston Post*. April 9, 1990, A-1.

"Rain or Shine, Play Ball." *Life*. April 9, 1965, 58:86–8.

Ray, Edgar W. *The Grand Huckster: Houston's Judge Roy Hofheinz, Genius of the Astrodome*. Memphis, TN: Memphis State University Press, 1980.

Root, Jay. "The Transformation of the Astrodome." *Houston Post*. August 13, 1992, F-10.

"Spreading Ideas: Domed Stadiums." U.S. *News and World Report*. September 8, 1975, v. 79, 45.

"Stadiums of the '60s." *Sports Illustrated*. July 10, 1967, v. 27, 36–7.

"Stadiums." *Architectural Forum*. September 1963, 119:96–103.

"Suddenly Everyone Wants to Build a Superdome." *Business Weekly*. December 5, 1983, 110.

Sutton, Horace. "Ball Players Under Glass." *Saturday Review*. March 6, 1965, 48:36–8.

Talbert, F. X. "Incredible Houston Dome." *Look*. April 10, 1965, 29:96–8.

"Under the Big Dome." *Newsweek*. August 17, 1964, 64:68–70.

# INDEX